There Really Is SAINT NICHOLAS

Written and Illustrated by
Bruce Kubski

Edited by Pam Zimmers
Cover Art by Lillian Kubski

ISBN 978-1-63844-561-6 (paperback)
ISBN 978-1-63844-562-3 (digital)

Christian Faith Publishing, Inc.
832 Park Avenue
Meadville, PA 16335
www.christianfaithpublishing.com

Printed in the United States of America

Lily's grandma and papa came for a visit on a cold, snowy afternoon.

"December is finally here, and Christmas will be coming soon," Grandma reminded Lily.

Lily was so excited! She'd been waiting all year for her favorite holiday.

"Santa Claus is coming! I need to write a letter to Santa!" she shouted excitedly. She gathered a pencil and paper and began her letter.

Just then, Lily's older brother, Alan, came home from school and asked Lily what she was doing.

"I'm making my Christmas list for Santa Claus!" she replied.

Alan laughed. "There is no such thing as Santa Claus."

Lily was very upset. "Santa *is* real, and he will be coming on Christmas Eve! He brings presents to all the good little girls and boys."

Alan scowled the way older brothers sometimes do. "There is no way that Santa could deliver toys to all the kids around the world in one night. It's impossible!"

This news devastated Lily, who started to cry. She went into the living room, where Grandma and Papa were visiting with Mommy and Daddy.

Daddy asked, "What's the matter, Lily?"

She replied that Alan told her that Santa Claus isn't real. With tears in her eyes, she asked, "Is it true? There's no Santa?"

Daddy sat Lily on his lap. "I believe in Santa," he reassured her with a warm smile.

"You're a big girl now, so you will understand the complete and real story of Santa Claus."

"A long time ago," Daddy began, "there was a very kind bishop named Nicholas. He helped people in need and had a legendary habit of secret gift-giving. He is also known as Nicholas the Wonderworker."

"And when that kind bishop passed away, he was rewarded for his work and kindness. He was made a saint, and people built the St. Nicholas Church to remember him."

Daddy continued, "Every year since then, he is remembered. Can you guess when?"

"Christmas!" cried Lily.

"Yes," answered Daddy, wiping away her tears. "That's when his spirit fills the air."

Daddy asked, "Do you know that feeling of excitement when you make or buy a special Christmas present for someone? What you are feeling is his loving, giving spirit—the true Christmas spirit."

"And, Daddy, why are there so many Santas around town?" Lily wondered.

Daddy explained, "That's someone dressed as Santa. But if that person truly has love for children and Christmas, then he has the spirit of Saint Nicholas in his heart."

"And that feeling of excitement you have on Christmas morning is also the spirit of Christmas in you."

Daddy continued, "I believe on Christmas Eve, Saint Nicholas makes a trip around the world and blesses all the Christmas gifts and everyone who believes. You see, Lily, I truly believe in Saint Nicholas because I feel his spirit in my heart just as I do God and Jesus."

Mommy assured Lily that she also believed in the spirit of Christmas, as did Grandma and Papa.

Alan, who was listening, apologized to Lily for losing his Christmas spirit. "I hadn't thought of it that way before. I really do believe in Santa and the magic of the Christmas season once again."

Lily gave Alan a great big hug and told him, "It's okay, you just didn't understand."

Alan wished Lily a merry Christmas and thanked her for bringing the Christmas spirit back to him.

"You see, Alan?" Lily grinned. "Santa Claus is also called Saint Nicholas, and he is the special spirit of Christmas."

"Merry Christmas to all!" cried Lily and Alan.

About the Author

Bruce grew up in a small-town suburb of Chicago. He was blessed to have been raised in a hardworking, loyal, loving home. Bruce has the great honor of being a husband and father to his amazing family.

Bruce hopes to help bring the spirit of faith and love into our daily lives. Imagine how life could be if we share our Christmas spirit every day. The joy of giving can be a simple smile or a kind gesture. Together we can help to bring peace and joy to the world.

Believe…

CPSIA information can be obtained
at www.ICGtesting.com
Printed in the USA
JSHW012110121122
33065JS00004B/124

9 781638 445616